SERIOUSLY GROWN UP
NO MACHINE ICE CREAM

A.J. Alexander

Copyright © 2017 by Anastasia Louise Johnson Alexander

All rights reserved. This book or any portion thereof may not be reproduced or used in any manner whatsoever without the express written permission of the author except for the use of brief quotations in a book review.

Photography Copyright © 2017 by Anastasia Louise Johnson Alexander

Cover Design by Matthew Rowett

This book is built on
a thousand words of encouragement
from a hundred dear people.

I might have tempted you in with ice cream,
but your support was the fuel I needed
to finally finish something.

Thank you all.

INTRODUCTION

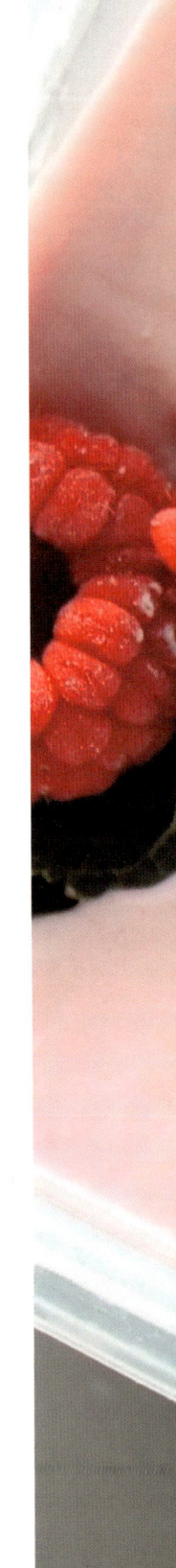

My love for ice cream - and most other things - spawned from laziness. I love to cook, and especially to cook for others, but when it comes to dessert time, there is no satisfaction like having it pre-made, waiting in the freezer.

The only problem is the stigma of ice cream. It tends to conjure up memories of children's birthday parties, as an aside to jelly, or plopped into a glass of cola or cream soda.

Or it is an accompaniment to a dessert - a scoop on top of a warm brownie, or melting into a crumble.

But ice cream can be a dessert in its own right, to which this book is proof.

All the recipes in this book work from the same simple combination of whipped cream and condensed milk. The magic of this method is that it freezes to smooth perfection, without the aid of an ice cream maker.

And not only does this recipe come with ease and simplicity, but it produces the richest, creamiest, most delicious ice cream.

I honestly don't know why anyone makes it any other way!

So it is cheap, all of the ingredients are readily available, and you don't need any complex machinery beyond some handheld beaters.

There is no excuse not to make your own delicious ice cream at home!

The possibilities for this ice cream method are not limited to this book. Whatever crazy - or ordinary, for that matter - flavours come to mind, you can make them a reality so easily with the simple base as your foundation.

So let's reclaim ice cream, and make it grown up, luxurious, impressive and - most importantly - absolutely delicious!

I sincerely hope you get as much enjoyment from making these ice creams as I have.

With love,
Anastasia

USING THIS BOOK

All the recipes in this book are "no churn", meaning they do not require the use of an ice cream maker or machine.

This book was written in the United Kingdom, and therefore uses ingredients and terms that may be unfamiliar to those who are not British. Where possible, alternatives are discussed either here or within the recipes.

All the recipes in this book call for the use of double cream, but this may come under different names, depending on where you live. If double cream is not available, heavy cream or whipping cream can be used as a substitute.

The main difference between these types of cream is fat content. Double cream is 48% fat, while alternatives can be as low as 30%. Try to obtain the highest fat content possible, to ensure the cream can be sufficiently whipped.

Condensed milk is sometimes called 'sweetened condensed milk'. The most well known brand is Carnation, but many major supermarkets sell their own brand as well. If you are unsure, the correct condensed milk is thick, and tastes very sweet.

Many of the recipes use biscuits, which you may know better as cookies. If you are unsure which type you need, think of what you might use to make the base of a cheesecake i.e. sweet and crunchy, without filling. In the USA, graham crackers are a good substitute for most of the recipes that call for biscuits.

The only two ingredients that are unlikely to be found in your local supermarket are lavender extract and violet essence, which can be purchased online, or may be found in specialist baking shops.

Unless otherwise specified, most of these recipes make approximately 1 litre of ice cream. This can vary depending on the volume of extra ingredients added. A litre of ice cream will produce about 6-10 servings.

The temperature of your freezer will determine how solid the ice cream freezes. A freezer around -18 degrees Celsius will, in most cases, produce ice cream ready to scoop. In a colder freezer, it may be harder and need 10-15 minutes to soften before serving.

CONTENTS

Classic Vanilla	13
Chocolate	15
Blackberry Ripple	17
Coffee	19
Salted Caramel	21
Cookies & Cream	23
Ginger	25
Turkish Delight	27
Banana and Peanut Butter	29
Spiced Apple Crumble	31
Blueberry Cheesecake	33
Eton Mess	35
Spiced Maple and Pecan	37
Cherry Bakewell	39
Pumpkin Pie	41
Green Tea	43
Earl Grey and Pomegranate	45
Cosmopolitan	47
Red Wine	49
Gin, Persimmon and Elderflower	51
Raspberry Mojito	53

Lemon and Rosemary	55
Lavender and Honey	57
Chocolate, Orange and Spiced Rum	59
Limoncello and Blueberry	61
Saffron and Vanilla	63
Fig, Honey and Ricotta	65
Pineapple and Tarragon	67
Violet	69
Maple and Crispy Bacon	71
Grapefruit and Roasted Beetroot	73
Strawberry, White Chocolate and Basil	75

CLASSIC VANILLA ICE CREAM

Who doesn't love a scoop of vanilla? It's timeless, fragrant and goes with anything. And if you are an ice cream novice, it is the best place to start. No frills or skills required - just delicious ice cream with minimal effort.

300ml double cream

200g condensed milk

2 tsp vanilla extract

1 litre container

Use handheld beaters or a freestanding mixer to whip the cream and the condensed milk together.

If you have whipped cream before, you will know when it is ready (about ten seconds after wondering if you have bought single cream, because nothing is happening!) once it starts to thicken, and forms soft peaks.

As always with whipping cream, be careful not to overbeat or you will end up with lumpy butter. Err on the side of caution, as under-whipped cream will still freeze well.

Add in the vanilla extract and stir in by hand. Have a little taste, and add up to a teaspoon more if you prefer a stronger taste.

Pour the mixture into your container and freeze for 6-8 hours.

CHOCOLATE ICE CREAM

You won't find a creamier, richer chocolate ice cream than this. Using real melted chocolate gives it a silky texture that can't be beaten. You will be making this classic flavour over and over again!

300ml double cream
200g condensed milk
100g dark chocolate
1 litre container

Beat together the double cream and condensed milk with a freestanding mixer or handheld beaters, until whipped and forming soft peaks, and then place to one side.

Break up the chocolate into small pieces and place in a heatproof bowl over a pan of simmering water.

Stir from time to time until mostly melted, then take off the heat and continue to stir until smooth.

Pour the melted chocolate straight into the cream and condensed milk, scraping as much from the bowl as possible. Use an oven glove to do this as your bowl will probably be quite hot.

Stir the melted chocolate in thoroughly until fully mixed, and then pour into your container.

Place it straight in the freezer and allow to freeze for 6-8 hours.

BLACKBERRY RIPPLE ICE CREAM

A slight twist on the traditional raspberry ripple flavour, this fruity yet creamy ice cream is bound to please. The ideal time to make it is towards the end of summer, when blackberries are at their best.

300ml double cream
200g condensed milk
2 tsp vanilla extract
250g blackberries
20g granulated sugar
1 litre container

Begin by putting the blackberries and the sugar in a small saucepan, with a splash of water - just enough to cover the bottom of the pan.

Place on a medium heat until the water is simmering, and then turn down low. The fruit will break down and make a rich syrup.

Make sure to stir regularly so it doesn't burn. You may also need to give the berries a little squash with a fork to help the juices escape.

After approximately fifteen minutes, strain the fruit to extract the juice, and leave to cool.

Beat together the cream, condensed milk and vanilla extract with a freestanding mixer or handheld beaters. Continue for several minutes until the cream forms soft peaks.

Pour the ice cream into the container. Then pour the fruit juice over the top.

Using a butter knife, stir the juice carefully into the ice cream. Be careful not to stir in too much, as you do not want to lose the ripples.

Place in the freezer and allow to freeze for 6-8 hours.

COFFEE ICE CREAM

Coffee ice cream is an Italian classic, and the perfect way to make ice cream grown up. Feel free to add more coffee if you prefer a stronger taste.

300ml double cream
200g condensed milk
3 tsp instant coffee
1 litre container

Place the instant coffee in a small bowl or cup, and add a splash of near boiling water to it.

Stir to ensure it is fully dissolved, and then set aside.

If you prefer a stronger flavour, you can use up to two additional teaspoons of coffee.

Beat together the cream and condensed milk for approximately three minutes, before adding in the coffee.

Continue to beat the mixture until it thickens and forms soft peaks.

Pour the ice cream into your container, and freeze for 6-8 hours.

SALTED CARAMEL ICE CREAM

Salted caramel is beloved due to the unbeatable mixture of sweet and salty. When added to ice cream, it is rich and delicious. There is no need for the condensed milk in this recipe, as the salted caramel provides enough sweetness.

360ml double cream

100g granulated sugar

50g salted butter

1 tsp sea salt

1 litre container

Place the sugar in a saucepan over a medium heat, stirring continuously until it turns golden.

Add in the butter and stir in quickly and carefully, before gradually adding 60ml of the double cream.

Continue to stir for another 1-2 minutes before adding the salt and then taking it off the heat.

Leave to one side to cool and thicken.

Once the caramel has reached room temperature, beat the remaining cream in a separate bowl, until it forms soft peaks.

Spoon the salted caramel into the cream and stir in thoroughly by hand.

Pour the ice cream into your container and freeze for 6-8 hours, or preferably overnight.

COOKIES & CREAM ICE CREAM

Unbeatably simple, this flavour becomes an immediate favourite with anyone who tries it, both adults and children alike.

300ml double cream

200g condensed milk

1 litre container

150g chocolate wafer cookies e.g. Oreos

Beat together the cream and the condensed milk until it thickens and forms soft peaks.

Place your cookies in a sealed plastic bag, and, using a rolling pin, crush them until there are no large pieces left.

Stir the crushed cookies into the whipped cream by hand, making sure to mix it well.

Spoon the mixture into your container, and freeze for 6-8 hours.

GINGER ICE CREAM

This recipe uses root ginger, which gives a lovely flavour throughout, plus a great kick of warmth. Use more ginger if you wish the flavour to be stronger.

300ml double cream

200g condensed milk

1 hand of root ginger

1 litre container

Cut off approximately 80g from the hand of ginger.

You can use a little more, depending on how fiery you wish the finished ice cream to be.

Peel all of the skin from the ginger, and then very finely grate it. It will become more of a pulp.

Place this to one side.

Beat together the cream and condensed milk until it thickens and forms soft peaks.

Add in the grated ginger, and stir well to fully incorporate it.

Pour the ice cream into your container, and freeze for 6-8 hours.

TURKISH DELIGHT ICE CREAM

So simple, and an absolute winner, this is a must-try for anyone who loves traditional rose flavoured Turkish Delight. I have made this flavour on request far more than any other, yet it couldn't be easier to make. Add a little pink food colouring, if desired, for a pretty pink blush.

300ml double cream
200g condensed milk
150ml rose water
50g dark chocolate
1 litre container

Beat together the cream, condensed milk and approximately half of the rose water for a couple of minutes.

Rose water can vary in strength, so taste at this point and add more if necessary, until you achieve the desired flavour.

Continue to beat the mixture until it thickens and forms soft peaks. If you would like, a little pink food colouring can be added at this point. Add in very tiny amounts until you achieve the desired shade.

Break up the chocolate and melt in a heatproof bowl over a pan of simmering water. Keep stirring until fully melted, and then take off the heat.

Spoon a third of the ice cream into the container and spread it out evenly so the bottom is totally covered.

Dip a spoon or knife into the melted chocolate, and drizzle roughly over the top of the ice cream in the container.

Spoon another third carefully over the top, spread it out, and drizzle some more of the chocolate over it.

Repeat with the rest of the ice cream and the chocolate, before placing the container in the freezer for 6-8 hours.

BANANA AND PEANUT BUTTER ICE CREAM

Banana and peanut butter is a great combination that works very well in ice cream, and is a delicious way to use up that last brown banana that no one wants! Whether you use smooth or crunchy peanut butter is up to your personal preference.

300ml double cream

200g condensed milk

1 very ripe banana

2 tbsp peanut butter

1 litre container

Peel, slice and mash the banana until completely smooth, and then set aside.

Beat together the cream and condensed milk in a separate bowl for a couple of minutes.

Add the mashed banana and the peanut butter, and beat for a few more seconds.

Taste the mixture, and add more peanut butter if desired.

Continue to beat the mixture until it thickens and forms soft peaks.

Pour the ice cream into your container, and freeze for 6-8 hours.

SPICED APPLE CRUMBLE ICE CREAM

Apple crumble is a firm favourite dessert in Britain. With crushed biscuits in place of crumble, and a little cinnamon to give the apples a more robust flavour, this ice cream holds its own as an alternative.

300ml double cream
200g condensed milk
2 apples
80g biscuits
20g granulated sugar
1 tsp ground cinnamon
1 litre container

Core, peel and slice the apples into small pieces.

Add the apples to a small saucepan with the sugar, cinnamon, and just enough water to cover the bottom of the pan.

Cook on a medium heat until it starts to simmer, and then turn the temperature down.

Leave to cook for 10-15 minutes, stirring from time to time, until the fruit has softened.

Remove from the heat and allow to cool.

Place the biscuits in a sealed plastic bag, and crush into crumbs with a rolling pin.

Beat together the cream and condensed milk until it thickens and forms soft peaks, before stirring in the apples.

Pour half of the ice cream into your container, and spread out flat. Sprinkle half of the crushed biscuits evenly over the top.

Repeat with the rest of the ice cream, and the biscuits.

Place the container in the freezer for 6-8 hours.

BLUEBERRY CHEESECAKE ICE CREAM

This ice cream is my personal favourite, and the incredible taste has to be experienced to be believed. Use some oaty biscuits, such as digestives, to get the perfect flavour to contrast the sharp blueberries.

300ml double cream
200g condensed milk
200g blueberries
1 tbsp lemon juice
20g granulated sugar
75g biscuits
1 litre container

Place the blueberries in a small saucepan with the lemon juice and sugar, and just enough water to cover the bottom of the pan.

Cook on a medium heat until it starts to simmer, and then turn down low.

Using a fork, crush the berries to help the juices escape. Stir occasionally to prevent the fruit from burning.

After 10-15 minutes, remove the pan from the heat and allow the blueberries to cool.

Place the biscuits in a sealed plastic bag and crush into crumbs with a rolling pin.

Beat together the cream and the condensed milk until it thickens and forms soft peaks.

Then carefully stir in the blueberries by hand.

Pour half the ice cream into the container and spread it out flat. Sprinkle half the crushed biscuits evenly over the top.

Repeat with the other half of the ice cream and the biscuits.

Place in the freezer for 6-8 hours.

ETON MESS ICE CREAM

The traditional English dessert of whipped cream, strawberries and meringue works fantastically well as ice cream. When strawberries are out of season, strawberry jam containing real fruit works well in their place.

300ml double cream
200g condensed milk
1 tsp vanilla extract
300g strawberries
20g granulated sugar
40g meringues
1 litre container

Slice the strawberries into quarters and place in a small saucepan with the sugar and a splash of cold water - just enough to cover the bottom of the pan.

Cook on a low heat, stirring from time to time to ensure it doesn't stick to the bottom of the pan. Once the fruit has softened, give it a gentle press to help it break down further.

After 10-15 minutes, remove the fruit from the heat and allow to cool to room temperature.

If you are using strawberry jam instead of real fruit, you can skip this process, and just stir it straight in as it is.

Place the meringue in a sealed plastic bag, and crush into small pieces. A spoon or a rolling pin will be too aggressive - you are much better off just using your fingers to break it up.

For this recipe, you can use home made or store bought meringue, but you may find store bought works better as it tends to be less "chewy".

Beat together the cream, condensed milk and vanilla extract until it thickens and forms soft peaks. Then, carefully stir in the strawberries and the crushed meringue, before pouring into the container and freezing for 6-8 hours.

SPICED MAPLE AND PECAN ICE CREAM

Not for the faint-hearted, this ice cream is super rich and indulgent, and ideal for those who love spices and sweetness combined.

300ml double cream
200g condensed milk
1 tsp vanilla extract
70g ginger biscuits
2 tbsp maple syrup
25g chopped pecans
1 tsp cinnamon
1 tsp ground ginger
1/2 teaspoon nutmeg
1 litre container

To begin, beat together the cream and condensed milk until the mixture is whipped and forms soft peaks.

Stir in the vanilla extract, and half of the cinnamon, ginger and nutmeg.

Place your biscuits in a sealed plastic bag and crush them with a rolling pin.

Add to the bag your chopped pecans and the other half of the cinnamon, ginger and nutmeg. Give the bag a really good shake to mix it all up.

Pour your ice cream into your container in layers. Cover the bottom with a layer of ice cream, drizzle over it with maple syrup, and finally sprinkle a thin layer of the cookie crumble.

Repeat until you have used all the ingredients up, finishing with a fairly thick layer of cookie crumble.

Place in the freezer and leave for 6-8 hours to freeze.

CHERRY BAKEWELL ICE CREAM

The flavour that started it all, it remains one of my favourites. The cherry ripple works magnificently with the almond amaretto flavour. It works just as well without amaretto liqueur, for those who prefer an alcohol-free alternative.

300ml double cream
200g condensed milk
1 tsp vanilla extract
200g cherries
20g granulated sugar
50g amaretti biscuits
1 tbsp amaretto liqueur
1 litre container

Beat together the double cream and condensed milk with a freestanding mixer or handheld beaters, until whipped and forming soft peaks.

Stir in the vanilla extract and amaretto liqueur (if using). Spoon the mixture into your container and place in the freezer for around an hour to part freeze it.

The cherries must be reduced to a compote first, or they would freeze as solid lumps. Halve and pit them and place in a small saucepan with the sugar, and just enough cold water to cover the bottom of the pan.

Boil the cherries on a medium heat until the water starts to bubble, and then turn down slightly. You don't want them to burn. Leave to simmer for up to 20 minutes, stirring occasionally. Then take off the heat and allow to cool to room temperature.

Place the amaretti biscuits in a sealed plastic bag, and crush with a rolling pin.

Remove the container from the freezer and, using a dessert spoon, pour the cherries on top. With your spoon, cut into the ice cream in arcs, pulling the cherries down into it.

Sprinkle the crushed biscuits in a thick layer on top, and freeze for 6-8 hours.

PUMPKIN PIE ICE CREAM

A favourite for the colder months, this dessert can now be enjoyed as ice cream, and all year round! This recipe makes quite a lot more ice cream than the others in this book, so ensure you have a container large enough.

300ml double cream

200g condensed milk

350g puréed pumpkin

75g biscuits

1 tsp cinnamon

1/2 tsp nutmeg

2 litre container

If you are making your own purée from fresh pumpkin, you must make sure to remove as much water as possible.

Cook the pumpkin by steaming, rather than boiling, and once cooked, use paper towels to sponge off excess moisture, before pureeing.

Beat together the cream and condensed milk until it thickens and forms soft peaks.

Add the cinnamon, nutmeg and pumpkin purée to the mixture. Stir well by hand to ensure the mixture is fully incorporated.

Place your biscuits in a sealed plastic bag, and use a rolling pin to crush them to a crumble.

Spoon half the ice cream into your container, and sprinkle half the biscuits over the top.

Repeat with the other half of the ice cream and biscuits.

Place the container in the freezer for 6-8 hours.

GREEN TEA ICE CREAM

An acquired bitter taste, this flavour of ice cream is very common in Japan, and in Japanese restaurants across the world. And it couldn't be simpler to make at home.

300ml double cream

200g condensed milk

3 green tea bags

1 litre container

Place the tea bags in a small bowl, and pour approximately 20ml of near boiling water over the top.

Allow to infuse for several minutes, before giving the tea bags a little press to help the flavour escape.

Remove the tea bags, and leave the tea to one side to cool.

Beat together the cream and condensed milk until it thickens and forms soft peaks.

If you like, you can add a little green food colouring at this point.

Add the tea to the mixture, and stir thoroughly to fully incorporate.

Pour the mixture into your container, and freeze for 6-8 hours.

EARL GREY AND POMEGRANATE ICE CREAM

A beloved English drink, Earl Grey tea translates beautifully to ice cream. For a lighter, more citrusy taste, try Lady Grey tea as an alternative. Use a little food colouring, if desired.

300ml double cream
200g condensed milk
60ml pomegranate juice
100g pomegranate seeds
3 Earl Grey tea bags
1 litre container

Beat together the cream and condensed milk until it thickens and forms soft peaks.

Halve the mixture and spoon into two separate bowls.

In a separate bowl or cup, pour around 20ml of near boiling water over the tea bags.

Use a spoon to squash the bags and release as much flavour as possible.

Remove the tea bags and allow the tea to cool, before pouring into one half of the whipped cream and condensed milk. Stir thoroughly and then set aside.

To the other half of the mixture, add the pomegranate juice and most of the pomegranate seeds, and stir thoroughly.

Spoon both flavours into your container simultaneously, ensuring they are blended together. Take care not to mix too much, and lose the separate flavours.

Sprinkle the rest of the pomegranate seeds over the top, and then place in the freezer for 6-8 hours.

COSMOPOLITAN ICE CREAM

Inspired by the classic cocktail, and possibly one of the simplest recipes in this book, this ice cream combines vodka with citrus and cranberry flavours to achieve a very grown up and refreshing dessert.

300ml double cream
200g condensed milk
150ml cranberry juice
60ml vodka
1 orange
1 lime
1 litre container

Beat together the cream and the condensed milk until it thickens and forms soft peaks.

Add in the cranberry juice, vodka and the juice of the lime, and stir well.

Remove the zest from the orange, and stir in.

Have a taste, and add a little more vodka if you wish.

Pour the mixture into your container, and freeze for 6-8 hours.

RED WINE ICE CREAM

An unusual but pleasant and mature taste, this ice cream is visually pleasing at the same time! The trick to getting this right first time is to not take your eyes off the wine as it reduces.

300ml double cream

200g condensed milk

500ml red wine

1 litre container

The first thing you need to do is reduce the red wine. Adding it straight to the ice cream base would make for very watery (and therefore very icy) ice cream.

To reduce the wine, pour it into a small saucepan and place over a medium heat. Once it starts to bubble, turn the temperature down.

Stir regularly while simmering for approximately twenty minutes, and from then on stir continuously. It won't take much for it to burn, so keeping it moving is important.

After thirty minutes or so, it will have reduced to a syrup. Take off the heat and place to one side to cool.

Meanwhile, use beaters or a mixer to beat together the cream and the condensed milk. Continue until the mixture forms soft peaks.

Once room temperature, pour the red wine into the ice cream mixture and stir thoroughly. Then pour the mixture into your container and freeze for at least six hours.

GIN, PERSIMMON AND ELDERFLOWER ICE CREAM

Persimmons, also sometimes known as sharon fruit, have a fantastic sweet taste that is perfectly matched with the woodiness of gin, and the subtle floral aroma of elderflower.

300ml double cream
200g condensed milk
2 persimmons
120ml elderflower cordial
60ml gin
20g granulated sugar
1 litre container

Remove the stem of the persimmons, peel and cut into small pieces.

Place the fruit in a small saucepan with the sugar, and just enough water to cover the bottom of the pan.

Cook on a medium heat until it begins to simmer, then turn down low. Stir from time to time for approximately twenty minutes, or until the fruit has softened and broken down. You may need to give it a squash with a fork to encourage the juices to escape.

Take the pan off the heat and allow the fruit to cool.

Beat together the cream and condensed milk until the mixture has almost thickened.

Add in the gin and the elderflower cordial and beat for an additional 10-15 seconds to fully incorporate the flavours.

Elderflower cordials vary in strength, so have a taste at this point and add more if necessary. Continue to beat until it forms soft peaks.

Stir in the persimmons by hand, and then pour the mixture into your container. Place in the freezer for 6-8 hours.

RASPBERRY MOJITO ICE CREAM

Just like the drink, this ice cream is fun, fresh and distinctive. It not only tastes wonderful, but looks wonderful too - and what more could you ask from ice cream?

300ml double cream
200g condensed milk
300g raspberries
20g granulated sugar
3 sprigs fresh mint
100ml white rum
1 litre container

Place the raspberries (saving a few for decoration) in a small saucepan with the granulated sugar and two sprigs of mint, and just enough water to cover the bottom.

Cook on a medium heat until it starts to bubble, and then reduce the temperature.

Within a couple of minutes, you should be able to smell the aroma of mint.

Have a little taste of the juices, and if the mint flavour isn't coming through very clearly, add some more leaves.

Leave to simmer for another ten minutes, stirring from time to time, until the fruit has completely broken down. Then take off the heat and allow to cool.

Beat together the cream and condensed milk until it whips and forms soft peaks.

Strain the fruit to remove the mint and raspberry seeds, ensuring you get as much juice through as possible. Add the raspberry juice to the ice cream, as well as the white rum. Stir them both in thoroughly.

Pour the ice cream into the container, and decorate with the remaining raspberries and a few torn mint leaves, before freezing for 6-8 hours.

LEMON AND ROSEMARY ICE CREAM

Lemon works fantastically well in ice cream, being fresh and not overly sweet. This recipe pairs the classic citrus flavour with the very versatile aroma of rosemary, providing a pleasing floral contrast.

300ml double cream
200g condensed milk
20g granulated sugar
2 unwaxed lemons
3 stems of rosemary
1 litre container

Begin by zesting the lemons. Collect the zest in a bowl and set to one side.

Slice the lemons in half and squeeze the juice from them into a small saucepan.

Add cold water to the pan - roughly the same amount in volume as you have in lemon juice. Add the sugar and the rosemary stems, ensuring the herbs are submerged to help the flavours escape.

Cook on a low heat, stirring from time to time to prevent the liquid from burning. You will be able to smell the perfume of the rosemary quite strongly as it heats.

After ten minutes, set the juice aside to cool.

Meanwhile, beat together the cream and condensed milk for approximately two minutes.

Add the lemon zest and continue to beat until it is almost thickened.

Strain the lemon juice into the ice cream mixture, and beat together for a final minute or two, until it forms soft peaks.

Pour the ice cream into your container, and freeze for 6-8 hours.

LAVENDER AND HONEY ICE CREAM

This recipe uses lavender extract for ease, although real flowers can be used if you are sure they are free of pesticides and pollution. Add a little purple food colouring, if desired.

300ml double cream
200g condensed milk
5ml lavender extract
2 tbsp honey
1 litre container

If you have chosen to make this recipe using real lavender flowers, you will first need to infuse the cream with the flowers.

Heat the cream together with 2-3 stems of lavender until it just starts to steam, and then allow to cool completely before moving onto the next step.

Beat together the cream and the condensed milk for approximately three minutes.

If you are using lavender extract as recommended, add around half of it in now. Beat for a few seconds, and then taste.

Continue to add the extract a few drops at a time, beating and tasting until it reaches the strength you desire.

Add in the honey, and then continue to beat until it thickens and forms soft peaks.

Pour the ice cream into your container, and freeze for 6-8 hours.

CHOCOLATE, ORANGE AND SPICED RUM ICE CREAM

This ice cream is rich, luxurious and very popular! For a child-friendly version, drop the rum for a treat that is just as delicious.

300ml double cream

200g condensed milk

100g dark chocolate

1 large orange

50ml spiced rum

1 litre container

Beat together the cream and the condensed milk until it thickens and forms soft peaks.

Zest the orange, before slicing it in half and squeezing out the juice.

Add both the juice and the zest to the beaten cream, followed by the spiced rum.

Break the chocolate into squares and melt in a heatproof bowl over a pan of simmering water, stirring from time to time.

Once completely melted, pour the chocolate straight into the ice cream mixture, removing as much from the bowl as possible.

Use an oven glove to lift the bowl, as it will likely be very hot.

Stir the whole mixture thoroughly to fully incorporate all the ingredients.

Finally, pour the ice cream into your container, and freeze for 6-8 hours.

LIMONCELLO AND BLUEBERRY ICE CREAM

This liqueur, native to southern Italy, is becoming more and more popular, and lends itself very well to ice cream. The sharpness pairs well with blueberries, and makes for a tangy and fresh ice cream.

300ml double cream
200g condensed milk
1 lemon
3 tbsp limoncello
150g blueberries
20g granulated sugar
1 litre container

Grate the zest from the lemon, and place to one side. Then cut the lemon in half and squeeze the juice into a small saucepan, with a splash of cold water.

Add the blueberries and sugar to the lemon juice, and heat on a medium temperature for approximately fifteen minutes, stirring from time to time. You may need to give the blueberries a press to help the juices escape.

Once the fruit has softened and reduced, remove it from the heat and allow to cool.

Beat together the cream and the condensed milk for approximately three minutes. Add in the lemon zest and the limoncello, and continue beating until the mixture thickens and forms soft peaks.

Stir in the blueberries by hand. Be careful not to stir too much, so you achieve a ripple effect.

Pour the ice cream into your container, decorating the top with some whole blueberries if desired, and freeze for 6-8 hours.

SAFFRON AND VANILLA ICE CREAM

A famously luxurious spice, saffron creates an ice cream that is the most impressive shade of gold, and has a rich and earthy flavour. With a bit of time required, but an extremely simple method, this ice cream is bound to impress.

300ml double cream

200g condensed milk

2 tsp vanilla extract

1 pinch of saffron

1 litre container

Pour the cream into a sealable container (or a bag will do, if secure) and throw in a generous pinch of saffron.

Give the container a gentle shake to submerge the saffron.

Leave the container in the fridge for up to 24 hours, giving it more gentle shakes every so often.

As time passes you should see the red colouring bleeding from the saffron, eventually turning the cream a bright gold.

After the cream has finished infusing, pass it through a sieve or strainer to remove the saffron threads.

Add the condensed milk and vanilla extract to the cream, and beat together until the mixture thickens and forms soft peaks.

Pour the ice cream into your container and freeze for 6-8 hours.

FIG, HONEY AND RICOTTA ICE CREAM

The flavour of this ice cream is so subtle and understated, but is delightfully creamy and unusual, making the most of the flavour of the figs.

300ml double cream

200g condensed milk

4 fresh figs

1 tbsp honey

2 tbsp ricotta

1 litre container

Beat together the cream and the condensed milk until the mixture thickens and forms soft peaks.

Remove the flesh from the figs and add straight to the mixture.

Also add in the ricotta and the honey.

Have a taste, and add a little more honey if desired.

Stir the mixture well to ensure all the ingredients are fully incorporated.

Pour the mixture into your container, and freeze for 6-8 hours.

PINEAPPLE AND TARRAGON ICE CREAM

The sweet acidity of pineapple is perfectly contrasted with the gentle peppery taste of tarragon, giving this unexpected combination of ingredients a robust and unique flavour.

300ml double cream

200g condensed milk

200ml pineapple juice

200g fresh pineapple

2 sprigs fresh tarragon

1 litre container

Pour the cream into a sealable container (or a bag will do, if secure) and add in the sprigs of tarragon.

Leave in the fridge for up to two hours, before removing the leaves.

Chop up the fresh pineapple into very small pieces, and set aside.

Beat together the cream and condensed milk until it thickens and forms soft peaks.

Add the pineapple juice and the chopped pineapple, and stir well to incorporate.

Pour the ice cream into your container, and freeze for 6-8 hours.

VIOLET ICE CREAM

Anyone who loved Parma Violet sweets as a child must give this ice cream a try, as it has an almost identical flavour. And with only a couple of steps, you can have it in the freezer in five minutes! Feel free to add some purple food colouring, if desired.

300ml double cream

200g condensed milk

5ml violet essence

1 litre container

Beat together the cream and condensed milk for approximately two minutes.

Add in half of the violet essence, beat for a few seconds, and then taste.

Add more violet essence if necessary, a few drops at a time, until you reach the desired strength.

If you are using food colouring, you can add it carefully at this point.

Pour the ice cream into your container, and freeze for 6-8 hours.

MAPLE AND CRISPY BACON ICE CREAM

A great autumn-appropriate treat, this recipe may be a little off the wall, but is a delicious meeting of sweet and salty flavours. Sprinkle the bacon on top as you serve the ice cream, as it will lose its crunch if frozen.

300ml double cream
200g condensed milk
1 tsp vanilla extract
4 rashers bacon
50ml maple syrup
1 litre container

The first step is to grill the bacon. I recommend using streaky bacon, as the extra fat will help you get it perfectly crispy.

Grill on both sides until all of the fat is thoroughly browned.

While the bacon cools, beat together the cream, condensed milk and vanilla extract until the mixture forms soft peaks.

Add in the maple syrup and stir in by hand, before freezing for 6-8 hours.

When you're ready to eat the ice cream, finely chop up the bacon into small pieces.

Serve up the ice cream, and sprinkle some of the bacon pieces over the top.

GRAPEFRUT AND ROASTED BEETROOT ICE CREAM

Neither beetroot nor grapefruit is for everyone, but when combined they create a flavour that brings out both of their sweetness, and just seems to work. And who can resist such a beautifully vibrant ice cream?

300ml double cream

200g condensed milk

2 raw beetroots

1 large grapefruit

1 litre container

Remove the stems from the beetroots and peel them.

Wrap them in tin foil, place on a baking tray and cook in the oven at 180 degrees Celsius, for approximately one hour, or until soft.

When cooked, open up the foil and allow them to cool completely, before using a fork to mash them.

Beat together the cream and condensed milk for approximately three minutes.

Add in the mashed beetroot and continue to beat until the mixture forms soft peaks.

Add the juice and the zest of the grapefruit to the mixture, and stir well until fully incorporated.

Pour the ice cream into your container and freeze for 6-8 hours.

STRAWBERRY, WHITE CHOCOLATE AND BASIL ICE CREAM

The strawberry and basil combo is one that works so well, it keeps popping up all over the place! This recipe adds in some white chocolate for some additional sweetness, and results in a lovely silky texture.

300ml double cream
200g condensed milk
100g white chocolate
200g strawberries
1 sprig fresh basil
20g granulated sugar
1 litre container

Begin by infusing the cream with the basil by heating them together in a small saucepan. Cook on a very low temperature, stirring regularly to prevent the cream from burning.

As soon as the cream starts to steam, remove from the heat and allow to cool to room temperature.

Strain the cream to ensure all the basil is removed from it, and then beat it together with the condensed milk until it forms soft peaks.

Melt the white chocolate in a heatproof bowl over a pan of simmering water.

Pour the melted chocolate straight into the beaten cream and stir well. Pour into your container and place in the freezer.

Cut the strawberries into quarters and place in a small saucepan with the sugar and enough water to cover the bottom of the pan. Cook on a medium heat until simmering, and then turn down low for an additional ten minutes.

Once cool, remove the ice cream from the freezer and stir the strawberries in carefully, before returning to the freezer for at least 12 hours.

INDEX

A
Amaretti 39
Amaretto 39
Apple 31

B
Bacon 71
Bakewell 39
Banana 29
Basil 75
Beetroot 73
Biscuit 31, 37, 39
Blackberry 17
Blueberry 33, 61
Brown sugar 31
Butter 21

C
Caramel 21
Cheesecake 33
Cherry 39
Chocolate 15, 27, 59, 75
Cinnamon 31, 37, 41
Coffee 19
Compote 39
Cookie 23
Cosmopolitan 47
Cranberry 47
Crumble 31

D
Dark chocolate 15, 27, 59

E
Earl Grey 45
Elderflower 51
Eton Mess 35

F
Fig 65

G
Gin 51
Ginger 25, 37, 41
Grapefruit 73
Granulated sugar 17, 21, 33, 35, 39, 51, 59, 73
Green tea 43

H
Honey 57, 65

J
Juice 43, 47, 55

L
Lady Grey 45
Lavender 57
Lemon 33, 55, 61
Lime 47
Limoncello 61

M
Maple syrup 37, 71
Meringue 35
Mint 53
Mojito 53

N
Nutmeg 37

O
Orange 47, 59

P
Peanut butter 29
Pecan 37
Persimmon 51
Pie 41
Pineapple 67
Pomegranate 45
Pumpkin 41

R
Raspberry 53
Red wine 49
Ricotta 65
Rose water 27
Rosemary 55
Rum 53

S
Saffron 63
Salted caramel 21
Sea salt 21
Seeds 45
Spiced 37
Spiced rum 59
Strawberry 35, 75

T
Tarragon 67
Tea 43, 45
Turkish Delight 27

V
Vanilla 13, 17, 31, 35, 37, 63, 71
Violet 69
Vodka 47

W
Wafer 23
White chocolate 75
White rum 53
Wine 49

Z
Zest 47, 55, 61, 73

Printed in Great Britain
by Amazon

34688352R00046